JUDE

RISE TO THE TOP

FOOTBALL LEGENDS COLLECTION

By

RICHARD DEES

Copyright © 2023, Richard Dees

All rights reserved. No part of this publication may be reproduced, distributed, or transmitted in any form or by any means, including photocopying, recording, or other electronic or mechanical methods, without the prior written permission of the publisher, except in the case of brief quotations embodied in critical reviews and certain other noncommercial uses permitted by copyright law.

ISBN: 9798869814838

Printed in United Kingdom

First Edition: November, 2023

CONTENTS

Dedication

CHAPTER 1: Early Life and Family Background

CHAPTER 2: First Football Memories

CHAPTER 3: First Steps on the Pitch

CHAPTER 4: Birmingham Academy

CHAPTER 5: Blues Rising Star

CHAPTER 6: Moving to Germany

CHAPTER 7: Making a Mark in the Bundesliga

CHAPTER 8: International Impact

CHAPTER 9: Big Transfer to Real Madrid & First Season

CHAPTER 10: El Clasico Hero

CHAPTER 11: Winning the Golden Boy 2023

CHAPTER 12: Personal Growth and Challenges

CHAPTER 13: Ambitions and Dreams

CHAPTER 14: The Role of Family in Jude's Journey

CHAPTER 15: Learning from Setbacks - Overcoming Injuries and Challenges

CHAPTER 16: The Evolution of a Playmaker

Trivia

Footy Joke Corner

Guess Who

Disclaimer

DEDICATION

To every young dreamer who has ever kicked a ball,

To the underdogs who rise, and those who stand tall.

To the fans, the families, the teams near and far,

This book is for you, wherever you are.

May you always find joy in the game's simple pleasure, And may your love for football be a treasure forever.

Richard Dees - Lifelong football fan

JUDE: RISE TO THE TOP

CHAPTER 1: EARLY LIFE AND FAMILY BACKGROUND

In the heart of England, in the bustling town of Stourbridge, a story began. A story of a young boy with dreams as vast as the sky and a love for football that knew no bounds. This boy was Jude Bellingham.

Born on June 29, 2003, Jude's earliest memories were tinted with the green of grass and the thrill of a bouncing football. His family was not just a typical household; they were a team, with each member playing a vital role in Jude's journey.

His father, Mark Bellingham, a dedicated police officer, had another role when he came home – he was Jude's first coach and biggest supporter. "Jude," he would often say, "remember, football is not just about using your feet. It's about using your heart and mind."

Jude's mother, Denise, was the backbone of the family. She juggled her responsibilities with a grace that left Jude and his younger brother, Jobe, in awe. "Boys, make sure you play fair and have fun," she would remind them, as they rushed out into their backyard, transformed into a makeshift football pitch.

Jude and Jobe would spend hours there, under the watchful eyes of their parents, learning the art of football. The sound of laughter, the cheer of small victories, and the occasional friendly squabble filled their home.

It wasn't just in their backyard that Jude's skills shone. At school, he was known for his lightning speed and clever moves. His teachers and classmates would gather around during breaks, cheering as Jude dribbled the ball with a skill well beyond his years.

One day, as the autumn leaves began to turn golden, a local youth coach happened to pass by the school playground. He stopped in his tracks, mesmerized by the young talent he saw before him. The coach knew right away that Jude was special.

The path to football stardom is never easy, but for young Jude, his journey was about to take an exciting turn. With the support of his loving family and his undeniable talent, the world of football was waiting to welcome its next young hero.

And thus, the story of Jude Bellingham, a boy with a dream and a ball, began to unfold, leading him to places beyond his wildest dreams.

CHAPTER 2: FIRST FOOTBALL MEMORIES

Jude's love for football began much earlier than most. As a little boy, he would watch football matches on TV, his eyes wide with wonder. His favorite pastime was playing football with his family, especially his younger brother, Jobe. Their garden transformed into a grand football stadium in their imagination, with each match more thrilling than the last.

"Jude, pass it here!" young Jobe would shout, running across the lawn. Jude, with a grin, would skillfully dribble the ball before passing it to his brother. Their parents, Mark and Denise, watched from the sidelines, cheering and clapping for every goal scored.

One day, while playing in the garden, Jude's dad set up small goals, and they had their own mini-tournament. "Alright, Jude and Jobe, today we're having our own Bellingham Cup," Mark announced with a smile. The boys' excitement was palpable as they prepared for their garden showdown.

The match was a close one, with both brothers displaying their budding skills. Jude, even at that young age, showed an understanding of the game that was beyond his years. His movements were precise, and his shots on goal were powerful. In the end, Jude won the match, but the real victory was the joy and laughter shared between them.

After the match, as they sat sipping lemonade, Mark said, "You know, Jude, you've got a real talent for football. But remember, it's not just about winning; it's about playing with passion and enjoying the game."

These early football experiences with his family were not just about playing; they were moments of learning and growth. Jude's parents instilled in him the values of sportsmanship, teamwork, and the importance of enjoying the game.

At school, Jude's passion for football continued to grow. He was often seen playing with his classmates during breaks, his feet dancing with the ball. He had a natural leadership quality, organizing games and encouraging his friends.

His primary school teacher, Mrs. James, recognized Jude's talent. "Jude, you have a gift," she once told him. "But always remember to balance your studies and football. Both are important."

Jude took her advice to heart. He worked hard in class and on the football field. His dedication to both was evident, and he became a role model for his classmates.

These early years were crucial in shaping Jude's character and his approach to football. He learned the joy of playing, the value of hard work, and the importance of balancing different aspects of life. These lessons, learned on the playground and in the family garden, laid the foundation for the extraordinary journey that was to follow.

CHAPTER 3: FIRST STEPS ON THE PITCH

As the leaves fell and the chill of winter approached, Jude's extraordinary talent on the school playground caught the eye of more than just his classmates and teachers. The local youth coach, Mr. Thompson, who had witnessed Jude's skills, couldn't wait to talk to his parents.

One evening, Mr. Thompson visited the Bellingham household. Sitting in their cozy living room, he spoke with excitement, "Jude has a natural talent for football. I've seen many youngsters play, but Jude… he's different. He has the potential to be something special."

Jude's eyes sparkled with excitement, but it was his father who asked the important question, "What do you suggest we do, Mr. Thompson?"

"I'd like to invite Jude to join our youth team. We train young talents like him, give them the platform they need to shine," Mr. Thompson replied.

Jude's journey in youth football began with that crucial meeting. He joined the local youth team, where he trained rigorously, honing his skills and understanding of the game. His parents watched proudly as their son grew from a backyard football enthusiast to a budding star on the youth team.

The training was tough, and the matches were challenging, but Jude thrived. His ability to read the game, coupled with his agility and speed, made him stand out even among the most talented players.

One memorable match, the team was trailing by one goal. The atmosphere was tense, and the clock was ticking down. Jude received the ball in midfield, looked up, and with a burst of speed, weaved through the opponents. As he approached the goal, with only the goalkeeper to beat, he remembered his father's words, "Use your heart and mind."

With a swift kick, Jude sent the ball soaring into the net, scoring the equalizer and saving the game. The crowd erupted in cheers, and his teammates rushed to congratulate him. It was a moment that stayed with Jude, a testament to his growing prowess on the field.

As Jude's reputation grew, so did the attention from bigger clubs. Scouts from renowned teams started attending his games, keen to witness the young talent everyone was talking about. Jude, however, remained focused on his game, knowing that every match was a step towards his dream.

Meanwhile, at school, Jude was not just known for his football skills. He was a bright student, well-liked by his peers and teachers. Balancing academics and football was not easy, but Jude managed it with determination and support from his family.

As the seasons changed, so did Jude's journey in football. From playing in the backyard with his brother to becoming a star in the youth leagues, Jude Bellingham's early years were filled with challenges, triumphs, and the unwavering support of his family. Little did he know, this was just the beginning of an incredible journey that would take him to some of the biggest stages in world football.

CHAPTER 4: BIRMINGHAM ACADEMY

Jude's journey in youth football was like a storybook adventure. At just seven years old, he joined Birmingham City's youth academy, a place where his dreams of becoming a professional footballer began to take shape. The academy was a world of new challenges and opportunities, a place where Jude could hone his skills and learn the finer nuances of the game.

The academy's training ground was where Jude spent most of his days, practicing tirelessly.

"Keep your eyes on the ball, Jude," his coach would often say. Jude, determined to improve, would nod and continue with renewed vigour.

His talent was undeniable. He was not the tallest or the strongest, but his speed, agility, and understanding of the game made him stand out. Jude quickly became one of the top players in the academy, known for his ability to read the game and make decisive passes.

At the academy, Jude also learned the importance of teamwork. "Football is not just about individual talent; it's about how well you play with your team," his coach reminded them. Jude took this to heart, always ensuring he was a team player, both on and off the pitch.

One of the highlights of his time at the academy was a tournament where teams from all over the country came to compete. It was a big event, and Jude was both nervous and excited. The night before the tournament, he couldn't sleep. He lay in bed, thinking about the matches.

The tournament day arrived, and the air was filled with excitement and anticipation. Jude played exceptionally well, scoring goals and making crucial assists. His performance caught the eye of everyone present. In the final match, with the score tied and only minutes left, Jude received the ball. With a swift move, he dodged a defender and scored the winning goal.

The crowd erupted in cheers, and his teammates lifted him on their shoulders. It was a moment of triumph, a testament to his hard work and dedication. Jude's parents, who were in the stands, had tears of joy in their eyes. They knew their son was on his way to achieving great things.

After the tournament, Jude's coach pulled him aside. "You've got a bright future ahead of you, Jude. Keep working hard, and you'll go far," he said.

Jude's time at the Birmingham City youth academy was more than just about playing football. It was about growth, learning, and laying the groundwork for a career that would soon take the world by storm. Jude's journey had only just begun, but he was already showing signs of the football superstar he was destined to become.

CHAPTER 5: BLUES RISING STAR

Jude's journey at Birmingham City was like a rocket soaring into the sky – fast and spectacular. As he grew older, his skills on the football field became more refined, and his understanding of the game deepened. His dedication and hard work paid off when, at the age of 16, he made his debut for Birmingham City's first team, becoming the club's youngest ever first-team player.

The day of his debut was a whirlwind of emotions. Jude felt a mix of nerves and excitement as he put on the Birmingham City jersey with his name on the back. "You've earned this, Jude. Go out there and show them what you can do," his coach said, patting him on the back.

As Jude stepped onto the pitch, the crowd cheered. He could feel the energy and excitement in the air. The game was a blur of movement, with Jude seamlessly fitting into the team's rhythm. His confidence grew with every touch of the ball.

In one memorable moment, Jude received the ball in midfield, dodged a defender with a clever turn, and made a perfect pass that led to a goal.

The crowd roared in approval. Jude's debut was more than just a game; it was the beginning of his journey as a professional footballer.

Off the pitch, Jude remained grounded and focused. He continued to work hard in training and was always eager to learn and improve. His teammates admired his humility and work ethic. "Jude is not just a fantastic player; he's a great team member," one of his teammates said.

Jude's impact at Birmingham City was significant. He played with a maturity and skill that belied his age. Fans quickly took notice of the young midfielder who played with such passion and skill.

Jude became a symbol of hope and excitement for the club.

As the season progressed, Jude's performances continued to impress. He became known for his versatility on the field, able to play in multiple midfield roles. His ability to read the game, combined with his physical and technical skills, made him a vital part of the team.

Jude's time at Birmingham City was a critical period in his development. It was here that he proved he could compete at a professional level, facing older and more experienced players. His journey at Birmingham City laid the foundation for what was to come - a career that would soon take him beyond the boundaries of English football, to the grand stages of European football.

CHAPTER 6: MOVING TO GERMANY

Jude Bellingham's move to Borussia Dortmund marked a significant chapter in his footballing journey. Joining one of Germany's most prestigious clubs, known for developing young talents, was both an exciting opportunity and a substantial challenge for Jude.

As he set foot in Germany, the young star was filled with a mix of anticipation and determination. Adapting to a new country, with its unique culture and language, was an adventure in itself. "This is a new beginning, a chance to grow and learn," Jude thought as he embarked on this new phase of his life.

Dortmund's training ground became Jude's new arena, where he spent countless hours honing his skills. The style of play in the Bundesliga was different - faster, more physical, and tactically challenging. But Jude adapted swiftly, impressing his coaches and teammates with his work ethic and versatility on the field.

His debut for Borussia Dortmund was a moment of pride. As he donned the iconic yellow and black jersey, the cheers of the Signal Iduna Park crowd echoed in his ears. He stepped onto the pitch with a sense of responsibility and eagerness. In that match, Jude displayed maturity beyond his years, contributing significantly to the team's play and earning accolades from the fans.

Jude's time at Dortmund was marked by several memorable matches. He quickly became known for his dynamic midfield play, seamlessly transitioning from defense to attack. His ability to read the game, combined with his physicality and technical skills, made him a key player in crucial fixtures.

Off the field, Jude immersed himself in Dortmund's culture. He engaged with the fans, often staying after matches to sign autographs and take photos. His efforts to learn German and understand the local culture endeared him further to the Dortmund faithful.

Jude's growth at Dortmund wasn't just on the pitch. He matured as a person, learning to navigate the challenges of living abroad, dealing with the pressures of professional football, and embracing his role as a rising star in one of Europe's top leagues.

In Dortmund, Jude not only improved as a footballer but also left his mark as a beloved figure in the club's rich history. His journey at Borussia Dortmund was a testament to his talent, resilience, and the unwavering spirit of a young man chasing his dreams in the world of football.

CHAPTER 7: MAKING A MARK IN THE BUNDESLIGA

Jude Bellingham's journey with Borussia Dortmund in the Bundesliga was filled with record-breaking achievements and impressive performances that highlighted his rising star in world football.

Bellingham's debut for Dortmund on 14th September 2020 against MSV Duisburg in the DFB-Pokal was a remarkable start. At just 17 years and 77 days old, he scored the second goal in a 5-0 victory, setting records as the club's youngest goalscorer in the DFB-Pokal and their youngest scorer in any competitive match.

Following this, he marked his Bundesliga debut with an assist for Giovanni Reyna's opening goal in a 3-0 win over Borussia Mönchengladbach. His debut month's performances earned him the title of Bundesliga Rookie of the Month for September.

A historic moment came on 20th October when Bellingham faced Lazio in the UEFA Champions League group stage. At 17 years and 113 days, he became the youngest Englishman to start a Champions League match, breaking a record previously held by Phil Foden. He continued to be a regular presence in all competitions, showcasing his adaptability and skill.

One of his memorable Bundesliga goals came against VfB Stuttgart. In a tightly contested match, Bellingham equalised early in the second half, leading Dortmund to a 3-2 win. His performance in the 2021 DFB-Pokal final against RB Leipzig was pivotal in Dortmund's 4-1 victory, despite being substituted at half-time.

In December 2021, Bellingham played in the intense Der Klassiker against Bayern Munich. He made assists for both Dortmund goals in a nail-biting match that ended 3-2 in Bayern's favour. His performance, though overshadowed by the match's controversial moments, was a testament to his growing influence on the field.

The 2022 season saw Bellingham's role at Dortmund continue to grow. On 22nd October 2022, in a match against Stuttgart, he scored two notable goals – one from a rapid attack he started and finished, and another being a skillfully curved shot. These efforts were crucial in securing Dortmund's place among the league's top four.

Despite the challenges, including a knee injury that made him an unused substitute in the crucial match against Mainz 05, Bellingham's performances throughout the season were exceptional. His skills, dedication, and leadership on the field earned him recognition as the Bundesliga Player of the Season.

Bellingham's time at Dortmund was marked by rapid development, significant contributions to the team's successes, and personal milestones that established him as one of the most exciting young talents in football.

CHAPTER 8: INTERNATIONAL IMPACT

Jude Bellingham's ascent as a promising young talent reached a new pinnacle with his participation in the 2022 FIFA World Cup with England. His performances at Borussia Dortmund had already put him in the spotlight, but it was in Qatar where he truly showcased his extraordinary abilities on the global stage.

At just 19 years old, Jude's impact in the World Cup was immediate and profound. In England's opening match against Iran on 21st November 2022, he scored a brilliant header, marking the first goal in a resounding 6-2 victory. This goal etched his name in the record books as the first player born in the 21st century to score in a men's World Cup, and he became the second youngest player ever to score for England in the tournament.

Reflecting on his goal, Jude expressed his pride and joy. "I thought it had missed, as it took ages to loop into the goal but it was a brilliant ball from [Luke] Shaw and I just had to flick it away," he said. This moment was a highlight in his career, a blend of skill, timing, and execution that underscored his ability to make a significant impact in important matches.

In the World Cup, England's journey was marked by strong performances in the group stage, finishing first in Group B. The team demonstrated their prowess with convincing wins over Iran and Wales and a goalless draw against the United States. Jude's role in these matches was crucial, showcasing his evolving skill set and football intelligence.

Jude's contributions were not limited to scoring. In the second-round match against Senegal on 4th December 2022, he provided an assist, playing a direct part in the build-up to three more goals, underlining his significance in England's journey to the quarter-finals. His running skills, speed, and ability to exploit spaces made him a formidable opponent to even the strongest defenders.

The quarter-final match against France on 10th December 2022 was a tough challenge for England. Despite a valiant effort, the team was eliminated with a 2-1 loss. Jude's performance in this match was a testament to his growth and the experience he gained from playing at the highest level of international football.

Jude's achievements in the World Cup, coupled with his performances at Dortmund, where he had been on fire before the tournament, scoring nine goals and making three assists across all competitions, solidified his reputation as one of the most exciting young talents in world football.

CHAPTER 9: BIG TRANSFER TO REAL MADRID & FIRST SEASON

In June 2023, Jude Bellingham's footballing journey took a significant turn when Real Madrid announced his signing on a six-year contract. The transfer, with a base fee of €103 million potentially increasing to €133.9 million with add-ons, marked Jude as a significant investment for the club and a testament to his rising status in world football.

Jude's debut for Real Madrid on 12th August 2023 was a spectacle in itself. In an away match against Athletic Bilbao in La Liga, he announced his arrival with a goal from a close-range half volley. This debut goal set the tone for what was to become an extraordinary first season. In his second game, a 3-1 victory against Almería, Jude scored a brace and provided an assist for Vinícius Júnior, rapidly becoming the league's top scorer.

Jude's remarkable form continued, and he made a habit of scoring crucial goals, including a dramatic 95th-minute winner against Getafe in his first match at the Santiago Bernabéu. This feat made him the third player after Cristiano Ronaldo and Pepillo to score in each of his first four competitive appearances for Madrid.

His impact was not limited to La Liga. In the Champions League, Jude scored on his European debut for Madrid, securing a 1-0 home win over Union Berlin. His performance in these early European matches was a clear indication of his quality and potential on the continental stage.

By the end of October, Jude had scored 10 goals in his first 10 matches for Madrid, equaling Cristiano Ronaldo's record from 2009. His coach, Carlo Ancelotti, praised his performances, emphasizing how his goal against Barcelona completely changed the game.

Jude's adaptation to La Liga and his integration into Real Madrid's team were seamless. His ability to meet and exceed the high expectations set for him was a reflection of his talent, hard work, and determination. His first season at Real Madrid was not just about goals and assists; it was about adapting to a new league, integrating into a team with high expectations, and rising to meet those expectations.

Jude Bellingham's move to Real Madrid and his first season triumphs solidified his place as a key player for the club and a rising star in global football. His performances were a testament to his skills, adaptability, and maturity on and off the pitch.

CHAPTER 10: EL CLASICO HERO

Jude Bellingham's first season at Real Madrid was marked by many highlights, but none more memorable than his performance in El Clásico against Barcelona on 28th October 2023. This match, one of the most anticipated in the football world, saw Jude play a pivotal role in a dramatic 2–1 victory.

The Santiago Bernabéu Stadium was a cauldron of anticipation and excitement as the two giants of Spanish football faced off. For Jude, this was more than just a game; it was an opportunity to etch his name in the annals of one of the fiercest rivalries in football.

From the opening whistle, Jude's presence on the pitch was commanding. He displayed a mix of technical prowess and strategic intelligence, constantly posing a threat to Barcelona's defense. His movements were precise, his decisions quick, and his execution flawless.

The match's intensity was palpable, with both teams creating chances. It was a tightly contested battle, with Real Madrid and Barcelona demonstrating why this fixture is regarded so highly in the footballing world.

As the match progressed, Jude's impact grew. His ability to read the game and make decisive plays was a thorn in Barcelona's side. Then, in a moment that defined the match, Jude scored a spectacular goal. Receiving the ball at the edge of the penalty area, he skillfully navigated past a defender and unleashed a powerful shot that found the back of the net, leveling the score.

But Jude wasn't finished yet. In the dying moments of the match, with the score tied, he once again demonstrated his exceptional skills. Breaking away from his marker, Jude found himself in the perfect position to receive a cross from a teammate. With a precise and powerful header, he scored the winning goal, sending the

Bernabéu into a frenzy and securing a memorable victory for Real Madrid.

Jude's performance in El Clásico was a testament to his growing stature in world football. He had not only scored in one of the biggest matches of the season but had also played a crucial role in a significant victory for his team. His two goals, especially the dramatic winner, were a display of his exceptional talent and his ability to shine on the biggest stage.

Post-match, Jude's performance was the talk of the football world. Fans, analysts, and fellow professionals alike lauded his display, with many pointing to his performance as a defining moment in his career. His coach, Carlo Ancelotti, praised him, highlighting how Jude had changed the game with his skill and determination.

Jude's heroics in El Clásico were not just about scoring goals; they were about his overall contribution to the team, his tactical awareness, and his ability to rise to the occasion in high-pressure situations. This match in his first season at Real Madrid was a clear indication that Jude Bellingham was not just a rising star but a footballer capable of influencing the biggest matches in world football.

CHAPTER 11: WINNING THE GOLDEN BOY 2023

In 2023, Jude Bellingham's meteoric rise in the football world was recognized with the prestigious Golden Boy award, a testament to his exceptional talent and performances over the calendar year. This accolade, awarded to the best young footballer in Europe's top divisions, placed Jude among the elite group of players who have won this honor.

Jude's journey to the Golden Boy award was marked by consistent and remarkable performances, both at Borussia Dortmund and

Real Madrid. His ability to influence games, score goals, and provide assists was evident throughout the season. This led to his nomination and subsequent win of the award, an achievement that resonated across the football community.

Upon winning the award, Jude expressed his gratitude and excitement. "To be recognized with the Golden Boy award is an incredible honor," he said. "This is a testament to the hard work, the support from my teammates, coaches, family, and the belief they've all shown in me."

Jude's 2023 campaign was filled with individual highlights. At Dortmund, he had become a key player, showcasing his versatility and skill in the midfield. His performances in the Bundesliga and the Champions League were instrumental in Dortmund's successes.

After his transfer to Real Madrid, Jude's impact was immediate. He scored in crucial matches, including memorable performances in La Liga and the Champions League. His ability to adapt to a new league and team while continuing to perform at a high level was a key factor in receiving the Golden Boy award.

Analysts and former players praised Jude's development and the maturity he showed on the pitch. "Jude Bellingham has shown he's not just a promising talent but a player who can influence games at the highest level," commented a renowned football analyst. "His technical ability, combined with his tactical understanding, makes him one of the best young players in the world."

The Golden Boy award was not just a personal accolade for Jude; it was a recognition of his journey and growth as a footballer. It highlighted his evolution from a young talent at Birmingham City to a star at Dortmund and now a key player for Real Madrid.

Reflecting on his journey, Jude acknowledged the challenges and the learning experiences he had along the way. "Every step of this journey has been a learning curve. I've had to adapt, grow, and keep pushing myself. Winning the Golden Boy award is a milestone, but it's also a motivation to keep improving and achieving more," he said.

Jude's win was celebrated by his teammates, coaches, and fans. It was a proud moment for everyone who had been part of his journey, from his early days at Birmingham to his time in Germany and Spain. The award was a fitting recognition of his talent, hard work, and the bright future that lies ahead of him in the world of football.

CHAPTER 12: PERSONAL GROWTH AND CHALLENGES

Jude Bellingham's journey in professional football, while marked by remarkable achievements, was also a journey of personal growth and overcoming challenges. His transition from a promising young talent at Birmingham City to a star at Borussia Dortmund and Real Madrid was not just a professional evolution, but also a testament to his character and resilience.

At Birmingham City, Jude had already shown signs of his exceptional talent. But moving to Germany to play for Dortmund was a significant challenge. It meant adapting to a new country, a new culture, and a new style of football. "The move to Dortmund was a big step for me, both professionally and personally," Jude reflected. "It was about stepping out of my comfort zone and proving myself in a new environment."

In Dortmund, Jude faced the challenge of living away from home at a young age. He had to navigate a new language and immerse himself in a different culture. "There were moments of homesickness, moments where things were tough," Jude admitted. "But those experiences made me stronger, more independent."

Jude's move to Real Madrid presented a new set of challenges. The expectations at one of the world's biggest clubs were immense, and the pressure to perform was constant. "Joining Real Madrid was a dream come true, but it also came with a lot of pressure to perform at the highest level," said Jude. "It was about maintaining my focus, working hard, and living up to the expectations."

Off the pitch, Jude's growth was equally significant. He became known for his work ethic, humility, and the maturity with which he handled fame and success. His teammates and coaches at

Real Madrid praised his attitude and approach to the game. "Jude is an exceptional talent, but what sets him apart is his attitude," remarked Carlo Ancelotti, his coach at Real Madrid. "He's humble, hardworking, and always eager to learn and improve."

Jude's ability to adapt to different teams, leagues, and playing styles was a crucial aspect of his growth. He learned to adjust his game, understanding the tactical nuances and physical demands of the Bundesliga and La Liga. His versatility and intelligence on the field were a result of his willingness to learn and adapt.

The challenges Jude faced were not just about adapting to new environments. He also had to deal with injuries, intense media scrutiny, and the high expectations that come with being one of football's rising stars. "Dealing with injuries, the media attention, and the expectations were all part of the journey," Jude said. "It taught me about the mental aspect of football, about staying strong mentally and keeping focused on my goals."

Throughout his journey, Jude's family played a pivotal role. Their support and guidance were constants in his life, helping him navigate the highs and lows of his career. "My family has been my biggest support system," Jude shared. "Their belief in me, their advice, and their love have been crucial in my journey."

Jude's personal growth was as impressive as his professional achievements. From a young talent to a star at some of Europe's top clubs, his journey was a story of resilience, adaptation, and the relentless pursuit of excellence. It was a journey that not only shaped him as a player but also as a person.

CHAPTER 13: AMBITIONS AND DREAMS

Jude Bellingham's rapid ascent in the world of football, from his early days at Birmingham City to his pivotal role at Real Madrid, has been nothing short of extraordinary. However, beyond his current achievements lies a future filled with ambitions and dreams that Jude is eager to realize.

In interviews and conversations, Jude often reflects on his aspirations, not just in terms of trophies and accolades, but in terms of his growth as a player and his contribution to his teams. "My ambitions go beyond just scoring goals or winning matches. I want to be a player who makes a lasting impact, who helps to elevate the team and contributes to the game in meaningful ways," Jude shared in an interview.

At Real Madrid, Jude has set his sights on becoming an integral part of the club's storied legacy. "Being at Real Madrid, you're part of a club with a rich history. I want to add to that history, to be part of a team that writes new chapters in the club's story," he stated. His aspirations include leading Madrid to further domestic and European success, building on the club's impressive record.

Jude's ambitions also extend to his role with the England national team. Having already made a significant impact in international football, he dreams of playing a key role in bringing major trophies to his national team. "Playing for England has always been a dream, and I hope to be part of a generation that brings success and joy to our country," he expressed.

His personal goals are not just confined to his on-field achievements. Jude is passionate about using his platform to make a positive impact off the pitch. "Football has given me a voice, and I want to use it to make a difference, whether it's through charity work, inspiring the next generation, or addressing important issues," Jude commented.

Coaches and teammates often speak of Jude's unyielding drive and determination to excel. Carlo Ancelotti, his coach at Real Madrid, remarked, "Jude is a player with immense talent, but what really stands out is his desire to keep improving. He's never satisfied; he always wants to be better, and that's what makes him special."

Jude's dreams also include personal milestones, such as continuing to develop his skills, mastering different aspects of the game, and being recognized as one of the best players in the world. "Every player wants to be the best they can be. I'm no different. I want to keep pushing my limits, to see how far I can go in this game," Jude stated.

His journey so far has been a blend of hard work, talent, and a relentless pursuit of excellence. With his ambitions and dreams, Jude Bellingham is poised to not just be a star in the world of football but to be a role model and an inspiration for aspiring footballers everywhere.

CHAPTER 14: THE ROLE OF FAMILY IN JUDE'S JOURNEY

Jude Bellingham's ascent in the football world has been meteoric, but behind his success lies the unwavering support of his family. From his early days at Birmingham City to his stellar performances at Borussia Dortmund and Real Madrid, Jude's family has been a constant source of strength and inspiration.

"Family has always been my backbone. They've supported me every step of the way," Jude shared in an interview. This chapter delves into how his family's influence shaped his career, instilling values that go beyond the football pitch.

Jude's parents, Mark and Denise, played a pivotal role in his early development. Mark, a former police officer and semi-professional footballer, and Denise, a primary caregiver, provided a nurturing environment that allowed Jude's talents to flourish. "My dad's insights into the game and my mum's unwavering belief in me have been instrumental in my growth," Jude reflected.

Jude's brother, Jobe, also a talented footballer, has been both a companion and a competitor, pushing Jude to improve. "Growing up with Jobe, we always pushed each other to be better. Our backyard games were where it all started," Jude reminisced. This sibling rivalry and camaraderie played a significant role in his competitive spirit.

The move to Dortmund was a significant step for Jude, and his family's support was crucial during this transition. Adjusting to life in a foreign country at a young age came with its challenges, but the encouragement from his family helped him navigate this new chapter. "Leaving home was tough, but knowing my family was just a call away made all the difference," Jude stated.

Jude's family's influence extends beyond their support. They've instilled in him a sense of humility and the importance of hard work. "My parents always reminded me that talent alone isn't enough. It's about how hard you're willing to work for your dreams," Jude explained.

The impact of his family is evident in Jude's approach to the game. He plays with a maturity and level-headedness that belies his age, qualities he attributes to his upbringing. "My family has kept me grounded. They've taught me to handle success with humility and setbacks with grace," Jude commented.

Jude's bond with his family has remained strong despite the distances his career has taken him. They are regulars at his games, providing support from the stands. "Seeing my family cheering for me in the stands is the best motivation," said Jude.

As Jude continues to make strides in his career, his family's role remains central. "No matter where football takes me, my family is my anchor," Jude affirmed. Their influence has shaped not only the player he has become but also the person he is off the field.

CHAPTER 15: LEARNING FROM SETBACKS - OVERCOMING INJURIES AND CHALLENGES

Throughout his burgeoning career, Jude Bellingham has not only celebrated numerous successes but has also navigated through setbacks and injuries. Each challenge he faced provided a lesson and an opportunity for growth, shaping him into the resilient athlete he is today.

"Injuries are part of the game, but how you respond to them really defines you as a player," Jude once said, reflecting on the times he had to recuperate and bounce back. This chapter explores the challenges Jude faced and how he turned these experiences into sources of strength.

One of Jude's first significant challenges came during his time at Borussia Dortmund. A foot injury sidelined him for the first two matches of 2021, a period that was crucial for Dortmund's season. "Sitting out due to injury was tough. But it taught me the importance of patience and working diligently on my recovery," Jude explained.

His approach to recovery and rehabilitation showcased his professionalism and dedication. "The road to recovery was as much mental as it was physical. Staying positive and focused was key," Jude shared. His determination during this period was commendable and demonstrated his commitment to his craft.

Jude's journey has also been marked by the high expectations and pressure that come with being one of football's most promising talents. "Dealing with the pressure of expectations, especially after moving to Real Madrid, was a challenge. But I've learned to channel that pressure into motivation," Jude stated. His ability to handle pressure and use it as a driving force is a testament to his mental fortitude.

The transition from the Bundesliga to La Liga presented its own set of challenges, including adapting to a new playing style and team dynamics. "Every league has its unique style. Adapting to La Liga was a learning curve, but it's a process that has helped me grow as a player," Jude remarked on his adaptation to Spanish football.

Jude's coaches and teammates have often spoken about his ability to learn from setbacks. "Jude is a player who takes every challenge head-on. He learns, adapts, and always comes back stronger," noted Carlo Ancelotti, his coach at Real Madrid.

Off the field, Jude's maturity in dealing with the challenges of a high-profile sporting career has been notable. Balancing his professional commitments with personal life, dealing with media scrutiny, and maintaining his form amidst a packed football calendar are challenges he navigates with poise.

Jude's journey is a reminder that setbacks and injuries are part of an athlete's life, but it's the response to these challenges that defines a player's character and resilience. "Every challenge I've faced has taught me something valuable. It's about taking those lessons and using them to improve, both on and off the pitch," Jude reflected.

CHAPTER 16: THE EVOLUTION OF A PLAYMAKER

Jude Bellingham's transformation from a promising young talent into a dynamic playmaker is a story of technical growth, strategic understanding, and adaptability. This chapter will explore Jude's evolution as a midfielder, examining how his style of play has developed over time and the influences that have shaped him into the player he is today.

From his early days at Birmingham City, Jude displayed an innate understanding of the game. His youth coaches often remarked on his ability to read the play, make decisive passes, and control the tempo of the game. "Jude always had a vision on the pitch, even as a young player. He could see and execute plays that others couldn't," a former coach at Birmingham City recalled.

Jude's move to Borussia Dortmund marked a significant phase in his development. The Bundesliga's fast-paced and physically demanding style of play required Jude to adapt and evolve. He embraced these challenges, refining his skills and tactical understanding under the guidance of experienced coaches and mentors at Dortmund.

"In Dortmund, I learned a lot about the physicality and pace of the game. It was a different style compared to England, and I had to adapt my play accordingly," Jude commented on his time in the Bundesliga.

At Real Madrid, Jude's role as a playmaker took on an even greater significance. In La Liga, he honed his skills further, mastering the art of controlling the midfield, dictating the pace of the game, and providing both defensive support and offensive creativity.

"Playing in La Liga has been a fantastic learning experience. It's about understanding the nuances of the game and using your skills to influence the match," Jude shared about his experience in Spain.

Throughout his career, several matches stand out where Jude's capabilities as a playmaker were particularly evident. His performances in key Champions League matches and high-stakes league games showcased his ability to rise to the occasion and demonstrate his playmaking skills.

"Jude has the ability to change the game. His vision, passing, and tactical understanding make him a key playmaker for us," Carlo Ancelotti, his coach at Real Madrid, praised.

For Jude, being a playmaker is about more than just technical skill; it's about understanding the game and being a leader on the pitch. "Being a playmaker is about making the right decisions at the right time, understanding your teammates, and always thinking one step ahead," Jude reflected on his role.

TRIVIA

Theme 1: Real Madrid

1. What are the main colors of Real Madrid's home kit?

2. Which animal is featured in the Real Madrid club emblem?

3. What is the nickname of Real Madrid's stadium?

4. Can you name a famous player from Portugal who played for Real Madrid?

5. What is the special name given to matches between Real Madrid and Barcelona?

6. What country is Real Madrid from?

7. Real Madrid plays in which major football league?

8. Can you name one player who moved from Real Madrid to Juventus in 2018?

9. What is Real Madrid's training ground commonly known as?

10. Which Real Madrid player is known for his speedy runs down the wing and has a Brazilian name?

Answers:

1. White.

2. A crown (and a small dragon).

3. "The Bernabéu."

4. Cristiano Ronaldo.

5. El Clásico.

6. Spain.

7. La Liga.

8. Cristiano Ronaldo.

9. Ciudad Real Madrid or Valdebebas.

10. Vinícius Júnior.

Theme 2: Borussia Dortmund

1. What are the main colors of Borussia Dortmund's home kit?

2. Borussia Dortmund fans are famous for creating a huge 'wall' of which color in their stadium?

3. Can you name the Borussia Dortmund stadium where they play their home games?

4. Which country is Borussia Dortmund from?

5. Borussia Dortmund plays in which major football league?

6. Name a famous player from England who used to play for Borussia Dortmund.

7. What is the nickname of Borussia Dortmund's passionate fans?

8. Can you name the black and yellow bird that is also a symbol for Borussia Dortmund?

9. In what year did Borussia Dortmund win the UEFA Champions League?

10. What is a common nickname for Borussia Dortmund, based on their kit colors?

Answers: Borussia Dortmund

1. Yellow and black.

2. Yellow.

3. Signal Iduna Park (also known as Westfalenstadion).

4. Germany.

5. Bundesliga.

6. Jadon Sancho.

7. The BVB Fans or "Die Schwarzgelben" (The Black and Yellows).

8. The Bumblebee.

9. Die Schwarzgelben (The Black and Yellows).

Theme 3: Birmingham City

1. What are the main colors of Birmingham City's football kit?
2. Can you name the stadium where Birmingham City plays their home matches?
3. What is the nickname of Birmingham City Football Club?
4. In which city is Birmingham City located?
5. Birmingham City plays in which English football league?
6. Can you name any famous player who started his career at Birmingham City?
7. What is the mascot of Birmingham City, which is also a type of bird?
8. What year was Birmingham City Football Club founded?
9. What are the fans of Birmingham City commonly called?
10. Can you name the famous cup Birmingham City won in 2011?

Answers:

1. Blue and white.
2. St. Andrew's Stadium.
3. The Blues.
4. Birmingham.
5. As of 2023, they play in the English Championship.
6. Jude Bellingham.
7. Beau Brummie, a bull.
8. 1875
9. Bluenoses.
10. The Football League Cup (also known as the Carling Cup in 2011).

Theme 4: Jude Bellingham's Career Highlights

1. At which club did Jude Bellingham start his professional football career?
2. In what year did Jude Bellingham make his first-team debut for Birmingham City?
3. Which German football club did Jude Bellingham transfer to from Birmingham City?
4. How old was Jude Bellingham when he played his first match for Borussia Dortmund?
5. In 2023, which famous Spanish football club did Jude Bellingham join?
6. What position does Jude Bellingham mainly play on the field?
7. Can you name the international team that Jude Bellingham represents?
8. Jude Bellingham scored his first goal for England's national team in which tournament?

9. What special record did Jude set when he scored his first goal in the Bundesliga for Borussia Dortmund?

10. What prestigious award for young players did Jude Bellingham win in 2023?

Answers:

1. Birmingham City.
2. 2019
3. Borussia Dortmund.
4. 17 years old.
5. Real Madrid.
6. Midfielder.
7. England.
8. The 2022 FIFA World Cup.
9. He became Dortmund's youngest ever goal scorer in the Bundesliga.
10. The Golden Boy award.

Theme 5: Fun Football Facts

1. Which country won the 2018 FIFA World Cup?
2. What is the maximum number of players a football team can have on the field during a match?
3. Can you name the trophy awarded to the winners of the UEFA Champions League?
4. Who is known as the 'Egyptian King' in football?
5. What color card does a referee show to a player for a serious foul in football?
6. In football, what is it called when you score three goals in one match?
7. Which animal is often used as a nickname for the England national football team?
8. What do you call it when a player uses their head to hit the ball?
9. Which country is Lionel Messi from?

10. What is the name of the famous annual award given to the best male and female football players in the world?

Answers:

1. France.
2. Eleven players.
3. The European Cup.
4. Mohamed Salah.
5. A red card.
6. A hat-trick.
7. The Three Lions.
8. Heading.
9. Argentina.
10. The Ballon d'Or.

FOOTY JOKE CORNER

- What did the referee say to the chicken who tripped an opponent? *"That's a fowl!"*
- What's black and white, then black and white, then black and white again? *A Newcastle supporter tumbling down a slope!*
- I left two Everton tickets on my car dashboard yesterday. When I returned, someone had broken the window and left two more.
- Why was the football player sad on his birthday? *He received a red card!*
- What do you call someone who stands between goalposts and stops the ball from escaping? *Annette!*

- England's playing Iceland tomorrow. If they win, they're up against Tesco next week, followed by Asda.

- Which football team is a fan of desserts? *Aston Vanilla!*

- Where's the best place in the U.S. to buy a football uniform? *New Jersey!*

- What do Lionel Messi and a magician share in common? *They both can pull off hat-tricks!*

- The new coach of our struggling football team is strict. Last weekend, he caught two fans trying to leave early. He told them, "Get back in there and watch till the end!"

- Why did Cinderella get removed from the football team? *She kept avoiding the ball!*

- What's a goalie's favorite meal? *Beans on the post!*
- Why don't grasshoppers watch football? *They're cricket fans!*
- What's a ghost's preferred football position? *Ghoulkeeper!*
- Why did the coach bring pencils to the locker room before the match? *He was hoping for a draw!*
- Did you hear about the new Everton Bra? *Great support, but no cups!*
- Who was the top scorer in the Greek Mythology League? *The centaur striker!*
- What did the coach do when the field was flooded? *He sent in the subs!*

- My partner broke up with me because of my football obsession. I'm a bit down – we'd been together for three seasons.

- What ship can hold 20 football teams but only three leave each season? The Premier-ship!

- What's the difference between Bournemouth and a tea bag? The tea bag remains in the cup longer!

- Why was the world's best football player told to clean their room? *Because it was Messi!*

- Which part of the football field smells the best? *The scent-er spot!*

- Why did the football ball quit? *It was tired of being kicked around!*

- What do you call a Brentford fan after their team wins the Premier League? *Dreaming!*
- Why aren't football stadiums in space? *Lack of atmosphere!*
- Why do football players remind you of toddlers? *Both love to dribble!*
- God and Satan decided to settle their differences with a football match. God said, "All the good players come to heaven." Satan smirked, "But we have all the referees."
- Which football team has their tactics down? *The Hammers.*
- Why did the football player hold his shoe to his ear? *He loved sole tunes!*

- What's the coldest stadium in the Premiership? *Icy Trafford!*
- Which team begins every match with energy? *The Gunners!*
- What runs around the football field but never moves? *The sideline!*
- Which team is the stickiest? The Toffees!
- Best position if you don't like football? *Right back – in the locker room!*
- My computer caught the 'Bad-Goalie Virus'. *It can't save a thing.*
- Why did the football field turn into a triangle? *Someone took its corner!*
- Why did the football captain bring a rope to the field? *He was the skipper!*

- How do football players keep cool? *They stay close to the fans!*
- What do you call a Norwich player in the World Cup's knockout stages? *The ref!*

GUESS WHO

#1. In Madrid, he played, with a left foot so quick,

Scoring great goals, both strong and slick.

From Wales he hailed, with speed and with grace,

On the field, he'd often win the chase.

In Spain, he shone, with his hair tied back tight,

Can you guess this player, a true footballing knight?

#2. From sunny Brazil, with skills oh so bright,

A striker, a star, in the footballing light.

With fast feet and goals, he dazzled the crowd,

His footballing magic, bold and unbowed.

At Madrid, he starred, with his play so bold,

Can you guess who he is, this hero of old?

#3. In England, he started, scoring goals with a roar, at United and Everton, his legend did soar.

With strength and with spirit, he led the attack,

Now he's coaching a team, bringing his knowledge back.

In the city of Bellingham's rise to fame,

Can you name this player, known well in the game?

Answers:

1. Gareth Bale

2. Ronaldo #9

3. Wayne Rooney

DISCLAIMER

THE EVENTS AND DIALOGUES IN THIS BOOK ARE BASED ON TRUE INCIDENTS AND REAL INDIVIDUALS, PARTICULARLY FOCUSING ON THE LIFE AND CAREER OF BUKAYO SAKA. WHILE THE CORE EVENTS, DATES, AND ACHIEVEMENTS ARE FACTUAL, SOME DIALOGUES AND MINOR DETAILS HAVE BEEN FICTIONALIZED FOR NARRATIVE PURPOSES AND TO MAKE THE CONTENT ENGAGING FOR OUR TARGET AGE GROUP. ANY RESEMBLANCE TO PERSONS, LIVING OR DEAD, OR ACTUAL EVENTS IS PURELY COINCIDENTAL AND NOT INTENDED TO CAUSE ANY HARM OR MISREPRESENTATION. ALL RIGHTS TO THE NAMES AND LIKENESSES OF INDIVIDUALS, TEAMS, AND ORGANIZATIONS MENTIONED IN THIS BOOK ARE OWNED BY THEIR RESPECTIVE COPYRIGHT AND TRADEMARK HOLDERS. THIS BOOK IS MEANT FOR ENTERTAINMENT AND EDUCATIONAL PURPOSES AND NOT FOR COMMERCIAL EXPLOITATION OF THE NAMES INVOLVED.

Manufactured by Amazon.ca
Acheson, AB